...nothing is impossible
for pure love.
MAHATMA GANDHI

Always *and* **Forever**

(place your 4x4 photo here)

Our first photo of *you.*

Before You

A little bit about our family...

We spent our days...

Some of our favorite things to do together...

Our Journey to You

Why adopting you was important to us...

How we found you...

One thing we want you to know about your adoption...

Every child begins the world again...

HENRY DAVID THOREAU

It's a Match!

We were matched to you on ______________________ .

How we found out...

This is what we were told about you...

...the most astounding beautiful thing has happened here!

ALLEN GINSBERG

Your *name* ______________________

Your *birthday* ______________________

Who we told first...

How we celebrated...

We will
always
choose
you.

...all that we love deeply becomes a part of us.

HELEN KELLER

Our First Meeting

Where you were...

Things we could tell about you right away...

Seeing you for the first time was...

How we felt meeting you for the first time...

How we think you felt meeting us...

The best part of it all was...

A moment in my arms, forever in my heart.

UNKNOWN

The Best Decision

How we knew we were meant to be together:

Our first *family photo* **together.**

Counting the Days

From the time we decided to adopt till the day you came home,

it took ________________________ *(months/years).*

Waiting for you was...

We expected you to come on...

There were so many people who were excited to meet you...

And there were many people who helped us find you...

It's important to realize that we adopt not because we are rescuers.... We adopt because we are rescued.

DAVID PLATT

Getting Ready

We had so many things to do to get ready for you:

...I'm never not thinking of you.

VIRGINIA WOOLF

Dear child, I will care for you, protect you—until you are grown. And then I will let you fly free. But, loving you? That is for always.

CHARLOTTE GRAY

A Letter to You

Dear ____________________ ,

Love, ____________________

I take the pen and write: I love you so much, my heart is singing.

STEVIE SMITH

Welcome Home

You came home on ______________________ .

We were feeling...

____

____

____

____

____

____

You wore...

____

____

____

Some of your first visitors were...

______________________ ______________________

______________________ ______________________

______________________ ______________________

Home—home at last.

THOMAS HOOD

Your Room

We wanted your room to be...

We chose these colors:

And collected books such as...

Some special touches we added were...

This life is for loving, sharing, learning, smiling, caring, forgiving, laughing, hugging, helping, dancing, wondering, healing, and even more loving.

STEVE MARABOLI

Getting to Know You

We love watching you...

You are fascinated by...

Some of your favorite things are...

And the people you love to see are...

When you look at your life, the greatest happinesses are family happinesses.

JOYCE BROTHERS

Morning *routine*

Evening *routine*

Our life
will forever
be more
beautiful.

Where there is great love there are always miracles.

WILLA CATHER

Another Name for Love

You were born named: ______________________

We call you: ______________________

You call us: ______________________

Nicknames we have for you:

______________________ ______________________

______________________ ______________________

______________________ ______________________

Our First
year

The joys, the surprises,
the little miracles...

Our First & Second

Months Together

Ways you're changing:

You like:

We'll never forget:

____

____

____

____

____

____

____

____

____

____

____

____

____

You've grown ______________ *inches and gained* ______________ *pounds.*

I embrace you with all my heart.

ALBERT CAMUS

Our Third & Fourth

Months Together

Ways you're changing:

You like:

We'll never forget:

You've grown ______________ *inches and gained* ______________ *pounds.*

How strange, exciting and miraculous that we can change each other so much, love each other so much...

LAURIE ANDERSON

Our Fifth & Sixth

Months Together

Ways you're changing:

You like:

We'll never forget:

____

____

____

____

____

____

____

____

____

____

____

____

____

You've grown ____________ *inches and gained* ____________ *pounds.*

**Our job is not to tell children what to be,
but to show them the possibilities of being.**

HORATIO CLARE

Our Seventh & Eighth

Months Together

Ways you're changing:

You like:

We'll never forget:

____

____

____

____

____

____

____

____

____

____

____

____

____

You've grown ______________ *inches and gained* ______________ *pounds.*

You are the closest I will ever come to magic.

SUZANNE FINNAMORE

Our Ninth & Tenth

Months Together

Ways you're changing:

You like:

We'll never forget:

____

____

____

____

____

____

____

____

____

____

____

____

____

You've grown ________________ *inches and gained* ________________ *pounds.*

Time has a wonderful way of showing us what really matters.

MARGARET PETERS

Our Eleventh & Twelfth

Months Together

Ways you're changing:

You like:

We'll never forget:

You've grown ______ *inches and gained* ______ *pounds.*

We do not find the meaning of life by ourselves alone—we find it with another.

THOMAS MERTON

Looking Back

Your arrival has meant some big changes for us...

It's astonishing how short a time it takes for very wonderful things to happen.

FRANCES HODGSON BURNETT

Moments & Memories

During your first year with us, we started some new traditions...

We shared special moments together, such as...

Some of our hopes for the year to come are...

You don't find love, it finds you.

ANAÏS NIN

We should not be asking
who this child belongs to,
but who belongs to this child.

JAMES L. GRITTER

Celebrations

We celebrated your first birthday with us by...

You received well-wishes on your special day from...

Your favorite moment was...

...a happy memory never wears out.

LIBBIE FUDIM

Being With You

What it feels like to hold you...

What I see when I look in your eyes...

Things we like to talk about and say to you...

Some of the most special things about you are...

Hello to a new adventure.

ERNIE HARWELL

Favorite Things

Here are some of your favorite...

Foods:

Songs:

Books:

Movies / Shows:

Important Firsts

We've celebrated some memorable firsts together, including...

**We remember best what we love most,
and what is loved is always remembered.**

WARREN GODDARD

Adoption Day!

You were officially adopted on ______________________________

when you were ______________ *(months/years old).*

Who was there:

______________________ ______________________

______________________ ______________________

______________________ ______________________

______________________ ______________________

How we celebrated:

____

____

____

____

____

____

...we belong to each other.

MOTHER TERESA

Lessons of Love

We've learned so much through this journey.
Some things we want you to know...

Hopes & Dreams

More than anything, we want these things for you:

When we imagine you all grown up, we know you'll be...

We hope you'll always remember...

Remember that wherever your heart is, there you will find your treasure.

PAULO COELHO

Written and Compiled by: Amelia Riedler
Edited by: Nancy W. Cortelyou
Designed by: Jessica Phoenix

ISBN: 978-1-970147-65-0

1st printing. Printed in China with soy inks on FSC®-Mix certified paper.

Create meaningful moments with gifts that inspire.

...in the end it's love
and love alone
that really matters.
TOM ROBBINS